Machine Appliqué Made Easy

A BEGINNER'S GUIDE TO TECHNIQUES, STITCHES & DECORATIVE PROJECTS

JEAN WELLS

C&T PUBLISHING

Text © 2005 Jean Wells
Artwork © 2005 C&T Publishing, Inc.

Publisher: Amy Marson
Editorial Director: Gailen Runge
Acquisitions Editor: Jan Grigsby
Developmental Editor: Candie Frankel
Technical Editors: Ellen Pahl, Joyce Lytle, René Steinpress
Copyeditor/Proofreader: Wordfirm
Cover/Book Designer: Christina D. Jarumay
Design Director: Christina D. Jarumay
Illustrator: Tim Manibusan
Production Assistant: Kirstie L. McCormick
Photography: All photography by C&T staff
Published by C&T Publishing, Inc., P.O. Box 1456, Lafayette, CA 94549

Front cover: Designs from *Leaf Pillow* by Jean Wells
Back cover: Garden Chair cushion, *Moonlit Mountains,* and details from
Animals on Parade by Jean Wells

Library of Congress Cataloging-in-Publication Data
Wells, Jean.
  Machine appliqué made easy: a beginner's guide to techniques, stitches
& decorative projects / Jean Wells.
       p. cm.
  Includes bibliographical references and index.
  ISBN 1-57120-290-0 (paper trade)
 1. Machine appliqué. 2. Machine appliqué–Patterns. I. Title.

TT779.W4535 2005
746.44'5–dc22

                    2004017756

Printed in China
10 9 8 7 6 5 4 3 2 1

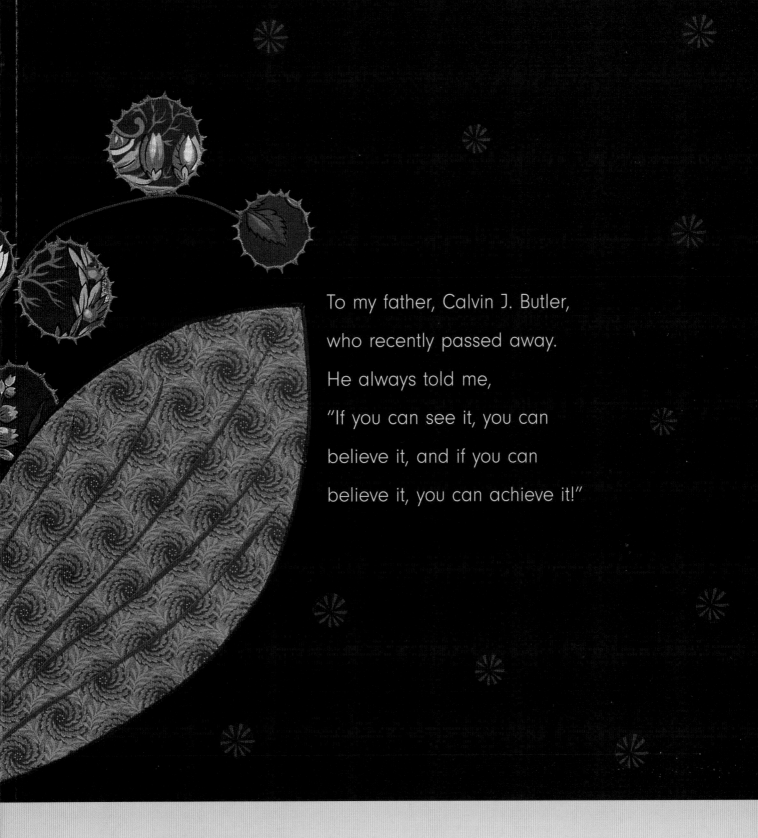

To my father, Calvin J. Butler,
who recently passed away.
He always told me,
"If you can see it, you can
believe it, and if you can
believe it, you can achieve it!"

Acknowledgments

Thanks to Todd Hensley, who asked me to consider writing this book for beginners. Working with the basics has been incredibly rejuvenating. Once again, I am honored to have Candie Frankel and Christina Jarumay as my editorial and design duo. My great appreciation also to technical editor Ellen Pahl, who made sure all the details were in place, and to the C&T team for making this project happen. They make being an author easier.

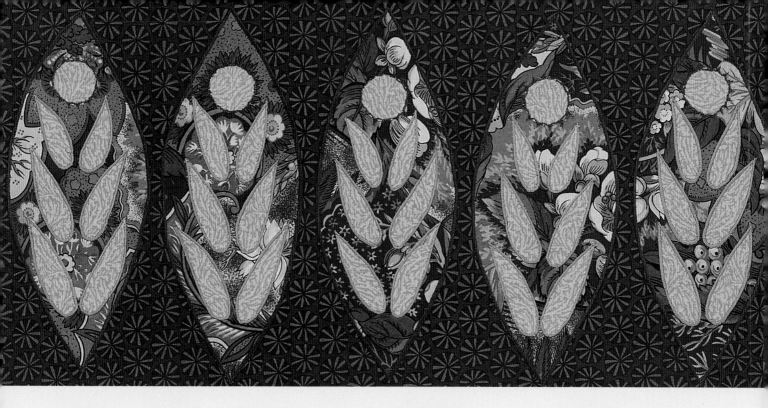

T A B L E   O F

CONTENTS

Introduction

Creating pictorial images on fabric continues to be one of my favorite sewing techniques. I started out 30 years ago, using appliqué in baby quilts. Today, I use appliqué in quilts and accessories to decorate my home.

An appliqué is defined as a cutout shape sewn to a larger piece of fabric. There are many ways to approach appliqué to achieve a desired effect. For example, the stitching can be decorative or it can be invisible. In this book, I focus on machine appliqué techniques that are fun to do and easy to master. I discuss machine stitches that are perfect for appliqué and explain how to make them work for you. Space-age products like fusible web and glue sticks are a must because they eliminate appliqué slipping and sliding once and for all.

The many beautiful quilting fabrics available in today's market make it more rewarding than ever to decorate our homes and lives by sewing. I designed the special collection of beginner projects in this book to help you get started. The patterns are interchangeable, which means that a zebra on a quilt would look just as great on a pillow. I also couldn't resist throwing in a few extra color palettes for even more inspiration.

I hope all of these techniques and project ideas motivate you to do wonderful things with machine appliqué. Enjoy!

Jean

Tools and Supplies

Fabric

Mood The fabrics you choose set the mood for your project. Think about the look you want to create and where and how the project will be used. Are you making a pillow for a particular sofa or room? If so, try to coordinate the pillow's colors and style with the existing decor. Use simple accents, such as pillows or wallhangings, to channel a neutral decor in a particular design direction. Similarly, when you sew a personal item, such as a tote bag, choose fabrics that suit the user's personality and tastes.

Contrast Strive for contrast in appliqué work. If there is no contrast between the background fabric and the appliqués, the design won't show. Fabrics that are too busy can also water down the design. Continue to audition fabrics until you find the best combinations.

The Joys of Cotton Cotton quilting fabric in a broadcloth weight is perfect for appliqué work. You may also use a slightly heavier, denim-weight cotton. Sewing on cotton is a pleasure, because the sewing machine needle glides in and out of cotton fabrics with ease. If you are concerned about the dye colors running, wash and press your fabrics before you sew. Most quilting cottons have 42" of usable width after prewashing; however, yardage requirements for the projects in this book are based on 40", so you will always have enough fabric to make the projects.

Build a Collection Many of the projects in this book use small pieces of fabric for the appliqués. Start collecting fat quarters (18" x 22") and small cuts of fabric in various textures, colors, and styles. It is easier to start a project when you can pull fabrics from your own collection.

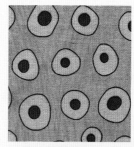

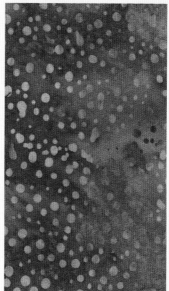
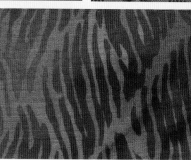

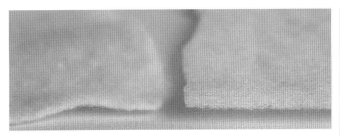

Select thin, lightweight cotton batting (left) for appliqué projects. It allows the project to lie flat, yet still gives the feeling of padding. Fusible polyester batting (right) is great for pillows and totes.

Thread

Color
Most of the time, it will be difficult to exactly match the thread color to the fabric. When you don't have the perfect color, choose a slightly darker shade, because it will blend in better than a lighter shade. Match the top thread to the appliqué and the bobbin thread to the background fabric. Use a contrasting thread color, however, when you want the stitching to serve as a decorative outline.

Type and Weight
Size 50 cotton thread (the kind used for general sewing) is the most common thread used in machine appliqué. You may also use polyester or rayon thread, for a smooth stitch with a little bit of luster. For blanket-stitch appliqué, choose a heavier thread, such as YLI Jeans Stitch or Mettler quilting thread, so that the stitches will show more effectively. For invisible appliqué, use a 0.004 nylon monofilament on top and a size 50 or 60 cotton embroidery thread in the bobbin. Choose clear monofilament for white or very light appliqués and smoky monofilament for darker fabrics.

Sewing Machine

For machine appliqué, you need a sewing machine with a zigzag stitch, a blanket stitch, and a blind hem stitch. Use the zigzag function for satin-stitch appliqué. Most machines that have the zigzag function can also perform the other stitches, as well as various decorative stitches. Use the blind hem stitch for invisible appliqué.

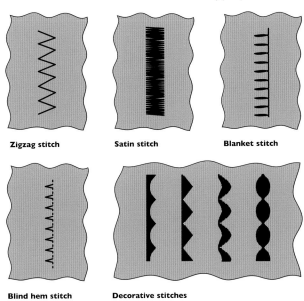

Zigzag stitch   **Satin stitch**   **Blanket stitch**

Blind hem stitch   **Decorative stitches**

Be sure your machine is well maintained. Machine appliqué creates a lot of lint from the thread; that lint collects in the bobbin area under the throat plate. I clean and oil my machine often.

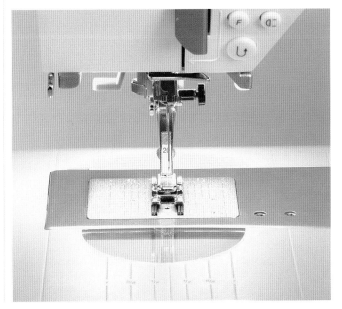

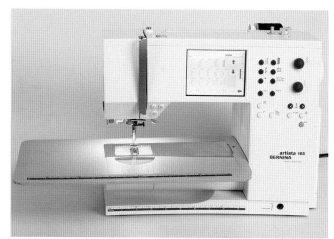
Zigzag sewing machine

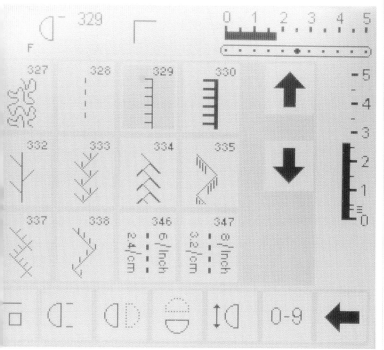
Control panel showing stitch options

NEEDLES

Begin every appliqué project with a brand-new needle. The needle size and type will depend on the thickness of thread you will use. Use this handy chart to find the appropriate needle.

THREAD	NEEDLE
Size 50 cotton	80/12
Size 50 polyester or rayon	80/12
Nylon monofilament	60/8 Microtech or Embroidery
Jeans Stitch	90/14 Topstitch

OPEN-TOE FOOT

An *open-toe foot* looks and works like a regular presser foot, except there is no bar to block your view. With the open-toe foot, you can see the fabric directly in front of the needle as you sew. Once you experience the added visibility, you won't want to go back to a regular foot.

If your sewing machine doesn't come with an open-toe foot, check the owner's manual to see if one is available. This is usually the foot recommended for satin stitch. If an open-toe foot is not available for your machine, create your own by using a small saw or serrated knife to cut out the center part of your machine's existing foot.

DARNING FOOT

The *darning foot*, sometimes called an embroidery foot, is used to stitch free-form or straight lines of decorative threads on stems, leaves, and other appliqués. Lowering the feed

dogs enables you to move the fabric from side to side and forward and backward, similar to free-motion quilting.

Open-toe foot, darning foot

Just for Appliqué

IRON

An iron is your frontline tool for fusible appliqué and freezer paper appliqué techniques. Any type of iron will do. Because fusible web products do vary, be sure to set your iron to the temperature recommended in the fusible web manufacturer's instructions.

FUSIBLE WEB

Fusible web is a thin sheet of paper with a web or a dotted grid of adhesive on one side. This product lets you fuse appliqué shapes to the background fabric to hold the appliqués securely in place as you sew.

The adhesive side of the paper is easily identified by its rough texture. Avoid heavy film adhesives as they can be very sticky to stitch through and can gum up your sewing machine. Instead, ask for a lightweight, "sewable" product. To prevent the fusible web from pulling away from the paper, always roll the web for storage.

APPLIQUÉ PRESSING SHEET

An appliqué pressing sheet is a heavy plastic film that can withstand high heat. Use a pressing sheet during fusing to keep the iron and ironing board clean of any excess adhesive. This pressing aid also allows you to compose an appliqué unit from multiple shapes by overlapping them and fusing them together—the pieces fuse to one another without sticking to the pressing sheet. You can then fuse these multiple pieces to the background fabric as a single unit. You can use one appliqué pressing sheet over and over again.

Fusible web, appliqué pressing sheet

FREEZER PAPER

Use freezer paper to make paper patterns for invisible machine appliqué. The waxy side of the freezer paper sticks to the fabric when pressed with a warm iron. Freezer paper allows you to cut the appliqués with extreme accuracy because the paper pattern hugs the fabric and does not shift. When the appliqué is complete, peel off the paper pattern and discard it.

 Freezer Paper to the Rescue

Use freezer paper to protect the ironing board cover during fusing operations. Place it waxy side down on the area you want to protect.

GLUE STICKS

Glue sticks are invaluable for holding appliqués in place without pins. Be sure to choose a washable or water-soluble product for easy removal. Extend the life of glue sticks by storing them in plastic zip-close bags in the refrigerator.

SCISSORS

You will need at least two pairs of scissors, one for fabric and one for paper. To cut appliqué motifs from fabric, use good fabric scissors with sharp points. Use your paper-cutting scissors to cut paper-backed fusible web and freezer paper.

STABILIZERS

A stabilizer helps you avoid puckers or distortion when stitching your appliqués by machine. Purchased stabilizers look like interfacing but tear much easier. You may also use ordinary typing paper or tracing paper. Place the stabilizer against the wrong side of the background fabric, directly under the appliqué. After the stitching is completed, tear away the stabilizer. Avoid iron-on stabilizers, as they are too difficult to remove.

SEAM RIPPER

A seam ripper makes it easy to remove a stabilizer after the appliqué sewing is complete. Insert the tip of the seam ripper under the edge of the stabilizer and run it along the edge of the stitches. Be careful not to cut the sewing thread.

Preparing the Appliqués

Fusing Technique

Fusible appliqué is perfect for beginners—it's quick, easy, and fun. It's also nearly foolproof. You'll be happy with the results and be encouraged to move on to new projects. Using these techniques, you can make custom accessories to decorate your home or gifts that are sure to please.

MARKING FUSIBLE WEB

A big advantage to using fusible web is that the appliqué pattern is drawn directly on the paper backing. There is no need to mark the fabric.

1. Place the fusible web paper side up on the appliqué pattern. Because the fusible web is lightweight, you will be able to see the pattern through it.
2. Trace the pattern outline with a pencil directly onto the paper backing. If you wish, you may use a ruler to draw straight lines and a compass to draw circles. Another way to mark circles when drawing your own designs is to trace around everyday objects such as jar caps and saucers.
3. If you are tracing several patterns, allow at least $1/2$" of space between them. Group together patterns that will be cut from the same fabric.

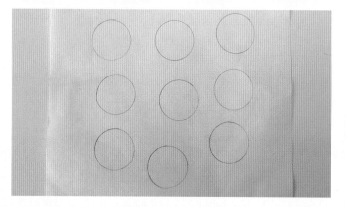

THE LOOSE CUT

Many projects require multiple appliqué shapes that use a variety of fabrics. To use your fusible web patterns on different fabrics, cut them apart into individual pieces.

1. Using paper-cutting scissors, loosely cut out each shape about $1/4$" beyond the marked outline. The cutting doesn't have to be precise for this step. Be sure to cut through the paper and the fusible web; do not separate the layers.

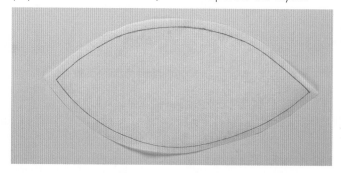

2. For a softer, more pliable appliqué, trim out the inside of the shape as well. This technique is especially appropriate for large appliqués or shapes that will overlap, as it helps reduce bulk and stiffness.

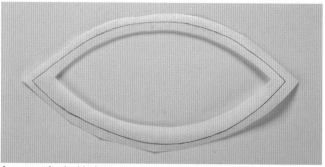

Loose cut leaf with the center cut away

3. Cut out shapes that will be cut from the same fabric as a unit.

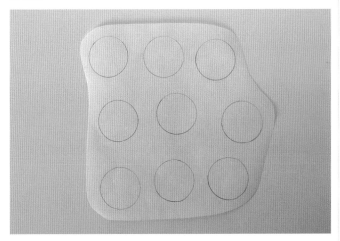

FIRST FUSING

Fusing is a two-step process. The first step is to fuse each shape to the wrong side of the appliqué fabric you have selected. Be sure to read and follow the fusible web manufacturer's instructions, as the iron temperature and length of time to press may vary from product to product. Here are some general directions:

1. Place the fabric right side down on the ironing board.
2. Place the pattern paper side up on the wrong side of the fabric. The rough side of the fusible web should be against the fabric.
3. Preheat the iron to the correct temperature.
4. Place the iron on the paper backing and press as directed, usually for about 5 seconds—just long enough for the web to fuse lightly.
5. Let cool. Do not remove the paper backing.

 Practice Makes Perfect

Fuse some extra appliqués for sewing practice. Random shapes cut from the fabric scraps are fine. Fuse the practice appliqués to a scrap of background fabric. Use these scraps to test your stitch style, stitch width, tension, and thread color.

THE FINAL CUT

Use fabric-cutting scissors to carefully cut out each shape on the marked line. If you have a lot of shapes, sort them into small piles by color or shape.

FINAL FUSING

Resist the temptation to jump immediately into fusing. Always do a dry run of your appliqué arrangement to confirm that the placement and colors are to your liking. Once you start fusing, you won't be able to make adjustments. Follow the general guidelines below. Review the manufacturer's instructions for your particular product.

1. Place the background fabric right side up on the ironing board.
2. Peel the paper backing from the wrong side of the appliqué to expose the fusible web.

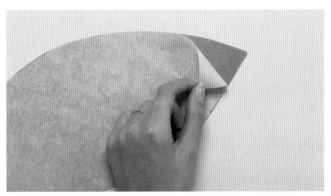

3. Place the appliqués right side up on the background fabric.

4. Preheat the iron to the setting recommended for your fusible web. Follow the manufacturer's instructions and press firmly. If the appliqué is large, lift and reposition the iron until the entire appliqué is fused.

Freezer Paper Patterns

Freezer paper patterns are used instead of fusible web for invisible stitch appliqué. The freezer paper has a waxy side that adheres to fabric when pressed with a warm iron. Think of it as a homegrown fusible.

1. Place the freezer paper waxy side down on the pattern. Trace the pattern outline. Use paper-cutting scissors to cut out the pattern.

2. Place the pattern waxy side down on the wrong side of the appliqué fabric. Press with a warm iron to adhere.

3. Use fabric-cutting scissors to trim the fabric $1/4$" beyond the edge of the pattern.

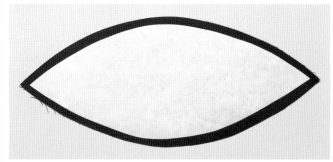

Wrong side

4. Roll the tip of a water-soluble glue stick along the edge of the pattern and the seam allowance. Finger-press the seam allowance onto the pattern.

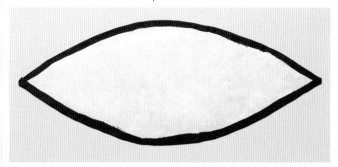

Wrong side with finger-pressed edge

5. Arrange the appliqués on the background fabric. Use pins or a glue stick to hold them in place for sewing. Refer to "Stitches", beginning on page 17, to machine sew your appliqués in place.

Right side

Beyond the Basics

The basic appliqué techniques are easy to master. Once you have mastered them, you'll be ready for just about anything, from overlapping designs to drawing your own. It's easy and fun. Be creative and modify the projects in this book, or design your own appliquéd quilts and accessories.

OVERLAPPING APPLIQUÉS

In many designs, the appliqués overlap to create a feeling of depth and dimension. There are two ways to fuse overlapping appliqués. Either way, remember to peel off the paper backing before you begin.

For simple designs, you will appliqué the pieces one at a time. Arrange all the appliqués on the background fabric, overlapping them as desired. Remove all the appliqués one by one, until only the bottom one remains. Fuse the bottom appliqué in place. Reposition the appliqués one by one, in the reverse order that you removed them, fusing each one in place as you go.

For complex designs, arrange the appliqués right side up on an appliqué pressing sheet. Be careful not to jostle the pieces or change their position. Press to fuse the pieces together. Let the pieces cool completely. Pull the design off the pressing sheet as a unit. This method is ideal for designs with lots of little pieces because you don't burn your fingers trying to fuse the pieces.

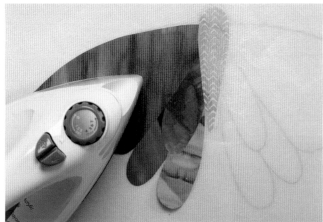

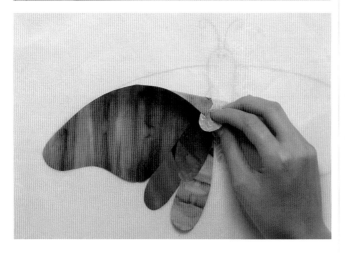

REVERSING THE PATTERN

You may have noticed that, in the course of the fusing process, every appliqué pattern reverses itself. To appliqué a zebra that faces right, you start by tracing a zebra that faces left. The patterns in this book are all mirror images of the way they appear in the finished project. Keep this principle in mind when designing your own appliqués, particularly for letters and numbers. For the final appliqués to read correctly, you must start out with backward letters and numbers. Of course, for symmetrical shapes, such as circles, this distinction does not apply.

DESIGNING YOUR OWN

I hope the projects in this book will inspire you to branch out and come up with your own appliqué designs and project ideas. Keep in mind that appliqués sewn by machine should have clean, simple lines. Curves are fine, as long as they are not too intricate. Avoid teeny-tiny pieces.

If you feel you can't draw, use tracing paper. Place the tracing paper over a photograph or a picture, and use a pencil to trace around a shape that interests you. You'll find that tracing paper blurs the details, which in turn forces you to keep the outline simple. You can create a lot of designs by tracing shapes you find in magazines, advertisements, and greeting cards. Use a copy machine or scanner to enlarge or reduce your drawings.

Stitches

Satin Stitch

THE LOOK

Satin stitch is a very closely spaced zigzag stitch. It creates a strong visual outline around the appliqué shape and makes for a very durable appliqué.

You can adjust the width of the satin stitch either narrow or wide. If your sewing machine has a movable stitch-width dial, you can actually change the stitch width as you sew. Refer to your sewing machine manual for details. I like to use this feature when I am stitching details inside a leaf, because it lets me taper the stitching line to a sharp point.

MACHINE SETTINGS

Start by setting your machine to a normal zigzag stitch. Consult your sewing machine manual to find out what stitch length the manufacturer recommends for satin stitch and adjust your machine accordingly. Set the stitch width according to the size of the appliqué—use a narrow stitch width for smaller, more delicate appliqués and a wider setting for larger appliqués. Place a stabilizer under the fabric and pin in place.

Test your settings by sewing on scrap fabric. Examine the thread coverage. If the thread matches the fabric, the coverage may be fine. If you are using a contrasting thread, you may need to make the stitches closer together to prevent the fabric edges from peeking through. I usually like to make the stitches a little bit closer than recommended, regardless of the thread color, so that the stitching truly does look like satin. When you find a look you like, jot down the thread type and machine settings for future reference.

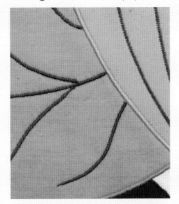

SEWING TIPS

⚙ Take time to practice your stitching technique on scrap appliqués. Concentrate on achieving even stitches and a smooth stitching line.

⚙ Use a tear-away stabilizer to keep the fabric and stitching smooth and flat. Cut a piece of stabilizer slightly larger than the appliqué shapes. Place the stabilizer under the appliqués, against the wrong side of the background fabric. Pin from the right side. After the appliquéing is complete, use a seam ripper to tear away the excess stabilizer.

⚙ Begin stitching on a straight or slightly curved edge. Set the needle to the far right zigzag position, and align it with the edge of the appliqué. Lower the presser foot and begin sewing. Guide the fabric by looking in front of the presser foot. If you look where the needle goes in and out, by the time the fabric reaches the needle, it's too late to make a correction.

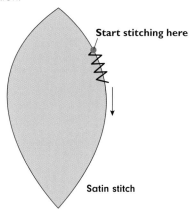

Start stitching here

Satin stitch

⚙ At an outside corner, stitch all the way to the end of the appliqué, right up to the new edge. Stop with the needle in the down position at the outside edge of the appliqué. Lift the presser foot and pivot the fabric. Lower the foot and resume stitching on the new edge. In tight areas, such as on the tip of a leaf, lift the needle and adjust the fabric position about two stitches' worth so that the new stitching does not extend beyond the appliqué.

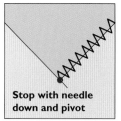

Stop with needle down and pivot

Outside Corner

⚙ At an inside corner, stitch past the corner for one stitch width. Stop with the needle in the down position on the inside edge of the appliqué. Lift the presser foot, pivot, lower the foot, and continue stitching. The new stitching will overlap the old.

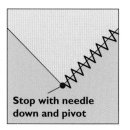

Stop with needle down and pivot

Inside Corner

⚙ After you have stitched all around a shape and reached the starting point, go over the previous stitches a short way to secure the edges.

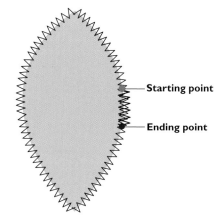

Starting point

Ending point

Overlap the stitches to secure the edges.

Outside Corner

Inside Corner

Satin Stitch Spacing
Satin stiches should be closer together than shown in the illustrations. Stitches are shown farther apart for clarity. See the photo details for closeups of actual satin stitching.

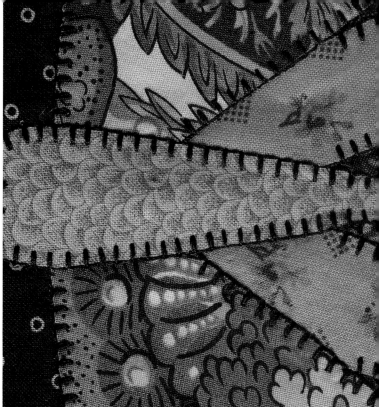

⊠ Pull all the loose threads to the back of the work. Tie off and clip. If a thread will not pull through, clip it close to the surface on the right side.

⊠ To satin stitch overlapping appliqués, begin with the shapes at the back and work forward, following the same order as you did for fusing. For example, sew flower appliqués in this order: stem, leaves, petals, flower center.

TROUBLESHOOTING

If your machine does not sew a smooth satin stitch, it may need a tension adjustment. The top tension can be loosened so the upper thread wraps around to the underneath side. If you have trouble with the tension, take your machine in for an adjustment and tell the mechanic what you are trying to accomplish.

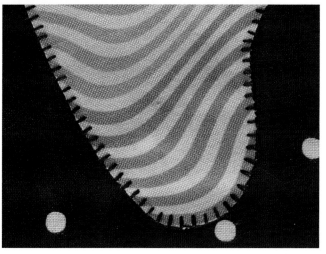

MACHINE SETTINGS

Consult your sewing machine manual for your machine's version of the blanket stitch. It may be classified as a hemming stitch, an overlock stitch, or an edging stitch. If you choose a thicker thread, be sure to use an appropriately sized needle as well. (See the chart on page 10.)

Start by setting your machine to a normal blanket stitch. Do a test run on scrap fabric to see if you like the look. As with satin stitch, adjust the stitch length and width. Changing the stitch length will increase the spacing between the little spurs. Changing the stitch width will make the spurs dip deeper into the appliqué. Choose a bigger, beefier stitch for large appliqués and a more delicate stitch for smaller appliqués. Jot down your settings once you find something you like.

Blanket Stitch
THE LOOK

Blanket stitch was a very popular hand-appliqué stitch from the 1800s up through the first half of the 1900s. It was usually worked in a contrasting thread color. Today, we call it a folk-art look. Machine blanket stitch simulates the hand-worked stitch, especially when a heftier thread, such as Jeans Stitch, is used. The stitching proceeds along the edge of the appliqué and dips in every third or fourth stitch.

SEWING TIPS

☒ Practice on scrap fabric. For a hand-stitched look, the outside stitches must fall exactly along the edge of the appliqué.

☒ Use a tear-away stabilizer.

☒ Begin stitching on a straight or slightly curved edge. Set the needle to the far right zigzag position and align it with the edge of the appliqué. Lower the presser foot and begin sewing. Guide the fabric by looking in front of the presser foot, not where the needle goes in and out. Be prepared for the needle to swing to the left every third or fourth stitch. Make sure the needle movement doesn't distract you; otherwise, the fabric may veer off course.

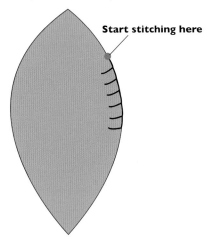

Start stitching here

☒ As you approach an outside corner, stop stitching and use the hand wheel for more control. You may need to manipulate the background fabric as well as the stitch to make sure you have a stitch exactly at the point. With care, you can turn a neat corner that resembles a hand-worked stitch.

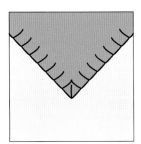

Outside corner

☒ At an inside corner, stitch toward the V until you have taken a stitch at the inside point. Again, you may need to manipulate the fabric a bit to place stitches where you want them. Leave the needle down, rotate the fabric, and begin stitching on the next side.

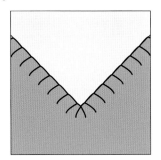

Inside corner

☒ For a clean finish, pull all the loose threads to the underside of the work. A gentle tug on the bobbin threads should be enough to pull the top threads through to the underside. Tie the loose ends together in a double knot. Trim the thread ends.

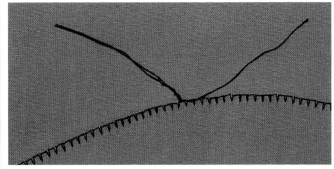

Wrong side

TROUBLESHOOTING

When using thicker threads, space your stitches farther apart and make them wider so that the stitch will be more defined.

Invisible Stitch

THE LOOK

The ingenious invisible stitch is an adaptation of the blind hem stitch, which is normally used for fashion and home decor sewing to give the look of a hand-tacked hem. In the appliqué version, the stitching is done on the surface using monofilament, instead of regular sewing thread. The needle makes a few straight stitches in the background fabric and a short zigzag into the appliqué, catching just one or two threads of the appliqué. The stitching is practically invisible.

The patterns for invisible stitch appliqué are cut from freezer paper, instead of from fusible web, and the raw edges are folded under (see Freezer Paper Patterns on page 14). This technique is well suited to large, simple shapes. Viewed from a distance, it looks like hand appliqué, but, of course, it is sewn in a fraction of the time.

MACHINE SETTINGS

Set your machine for a blind hem stitch, with both the width and length at 1 mm. Use a size 60/8 embroidery needle. Thread the machine with monofilament in the top and 60-weight embroidery thread in the bobbin. Practice stitching on scrap fabric.

SEWING TIPS

Use clear monofilament to sew light colors and pastels. Use smoky monofilament to sew dark colors.

Begin stitching with the needle close to the edge of the appliqué in a straight area, not at a corner. If the gap between the needle and the appliqué is too wide, the zigzag won't be able to catch the edge of the appliqué when it hops over.

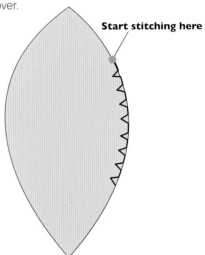

Start stitching here

Make sure the outside and inside corners of the appliqués are secure. Don't rush the stitching of these areas just because you can't see the thread.

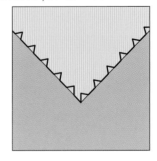

Outside corner

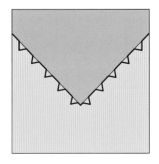

Inside corner

⊠ When you finish sewing an appliqué, turn the work over and trim away the background fabric, cutting $1/2''$ inside the stitching line. Dampen the exposed freezer paper pattern to soften it, and then remove the pattern. Press from both sides until the fabric is dry.

⊠ Sew overlapping appliqués one at a time. Remove the freezer paper pattern before moving on to the next piece.

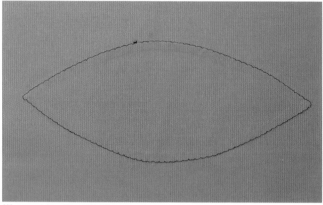
Wrong side after stitching

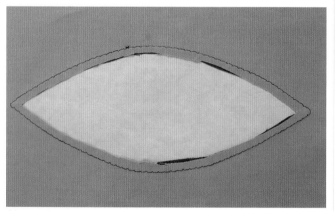
After cutting

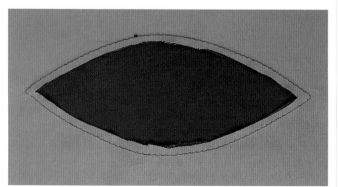
Freezer paper removed

TROUBLESHOOTING

⊠ To prevent the monofilament thread from spiraling out of control, place a "cot," a tubular piece of gauze, over the spool. You can find cots in the drug store near bandages and first aid items.

⊠ Try to glue and sew an appliqué in the same day. If the glue sets overnight, the freezer paper pattern becomes more difficult to remove.

Novelty Stitches
THE LOOK

Every zigzag sewing machine has a variety of decorative stitches that you can use to embellish appliqués. Sew a sampler of the different stitches that are available on your machine. When you are working on an appliqué project, don't automatically choose satin stitch. Take a look at your sampler stitches to see if there is one you might use.

Novelty stitch used for berries

Novelty stitch used for berries

MACHINE SETTINGS

Experimentation is the key to making the most of your machine's novelty stitches. Try different stitch lengths and widths. Also, try different thread weights, remembering to change to an appropriate needle size.

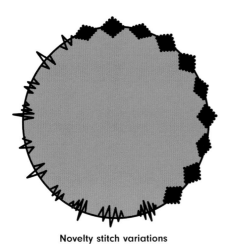

Novelty stitch variations

SEWING TIPS

Follow the sewing tips for the Blanket Stitch on page 20.

TROUBLESHOOTING

To prevent fraying, choose a stitch that covers the raw edges.

Do not use an elaborate decorative stitch on a print fabric. Doing so creates a look that is too busy. Think about how the stitch will appear on the fabric. Practice on fabric scraps first to check the stitch quality and appearance.

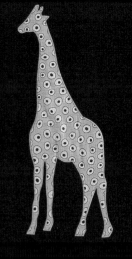

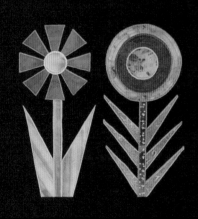

PROJECTS

Leaf Pillows

Pillow 1   12" x 12"

Pillow 2   16" x 16"

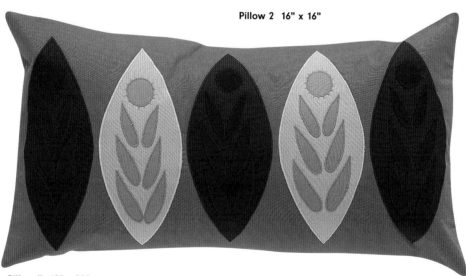

Pillow 3   12" x 22"

Appliqué a complete pillow collection with assorted leaves and berries. Mix and match the patterns as you like to get a coordinated look for your room. Satin stitching in and around the leaves adds decorative stylized veins and secures the leaves to the background fabric. A decorative scallop stitch creates a raspberry texture around the edges of red circle appliqués. The pillow covers, including the rectangular sofa pillow, are made in standard sizes to fit purchased pillow forms.

Materials

FOR PILLOW 1

$1/2$ yard light neutral for pillow

$1/4$ yard medium for leaves

$1/8$ yard accent fabric for berries

12" x 12" pillow form

FOR PILLOW 2

$5/8$ yard light neutral for pillow

$1/4$ yard each of 2 mediums for large leaves

$1/8$ yard dark for small leaves

$1/8$ yard accent fabric for berries

16" x 16" pillow form

FOR PILLOW 3

$7/8$ yard medium neutral for pillow

$1/4$ yard each of light and dark for large leaves

$1/8$ yard medium neutral for berries and small leaves

$1/8$ yard accent fabric for berries and small leaves

12" x 22" pillow form

FOR ALL 3 PILLOWS

30" x 36" piece of fusible batting

2 yards total lightweight fusible web

Thread to match appliqués

Cutting

	FABRIC	FOR THE TOP, CUT:	FOR THE BACK, CUT:
Pillow 1	Neutral	One 12$1/2$" x 12$1/2$" piece	Two 12$1/2$" x 8" pieces
Pillow 2	Neutral	One 16$1/2$" x 16$1/2$" piece	Two 16$1/2$" x 10" pieces
Pillow 3	Neutral	One 12$1/2$" x 22$1/2$" piece	Two 12$1/2$" x 13" pieces

Note: Cut a piece of fusible batting the same size as each pillow top.

Preparing the Appliqués

1. Using the leaf pillow appliqué patterns A–I on pages 54–56, trace the appropriate number of leaves and berries onto paper-backed fusible web. Group pieces that will be cut from the same fabric.

FOR PILLOW 1: Trace 2 of leaf A, 3 of berry B, and 5 of berry C.

FOR PILLOW 2: Trace 1 of leaf D, 1 of leaf E, 11 of leaf F, 4 of berry B, and 2 of berry C.

FOR PILLOW 3: Trace 5 of leaf A, 5 of berry C, and 10 each of leaves G, H, and I.

2. Loosely cut out the pieces and fuse them to the wrong side of the appropriate fabrics.

FABRIC PICKS

COMBINATION 1

COMBINATION 2

  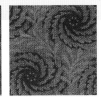 

COMBINATION 3

  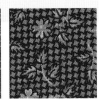   

Assembly

1. FOR PILLOWS 1 AND 2, use a pencil to lightly draw the vein lines on the right side of the leaves, as shown in the photographs and on the patterns. Study the leaves on houseplants or in a gardening book for additional veining patterns.

2. Stitch along the marked vein lines, using a narrow satin stitch and a dark, contrasting thread. If your sewing machine has a dial for stitch width, move the dial as you stitch, starting narrow and getting wider and then narrowing again. Practice on scrap fabrics before stitching on your leaf appliqués.

 Stitch First

The paper backing on the fusible web can double as a stabilizer. Work your decorative stitching on the appliqué with the paper backing still in place. Then remove the backing and fuse the appliqué as usual.

3. FOR PILLOW 3, fuse the smaller leaves and the berry to the larger leaf, using an appliqué pressing sheet. Then stitch the smaller leaves H, I, and J with a satin stitch and the berries with a decorative stitch, using the paper backing of the fusible web as a stabilizer.

4. Remove the paper backing and arrange the appliqués on the pillow tops, referring to the Appliqué Placement diagrams and photographs. Do a dry run to double-check the placement before fusing the pieces in place, following the guidelines below.

PILLOW 1: Place the leaves first. Then add the berries.

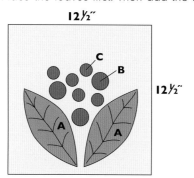

Pillow 1: Appliqué Placement

PILLOW 2: Position the 2 large leaves, overlapping as shown. Place the smaller leaves and berries. Let the larger leaves overlap 2 of the smaller pieces for added depth. Lightly draw 3 curving lines for the leaf and berry vines.

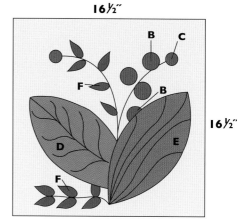

Pillow 2: Appliqué Placement

PILLOW 3: Center the first leaf on the pillow top in the middle, 1$^1/_2$" from the top and bottom edges. Place the remaining leaves on either side, alternating the colors.

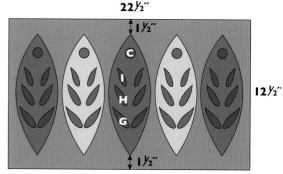

Pillow 3: Appliqué Placement

5. Stitch around the edges of the fused appliqués. See the close-up photos on opposite page for stitching suggestions.

Pillow 1: Add satin stitch around the leaves and a decorative stitch around the berries.

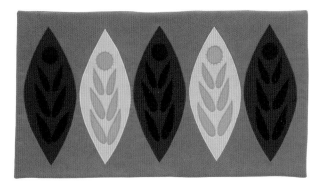

Pillow 2: Add satin stitch around the large leaves. Use a narrow zigzag stitch and contrasting thread to embroider the vines. Finish with satin stitch around the smaller leaves and a decorative stitch around each berry.

Pillow 3: Use satin stitch for all leaves and a decorative stitch around each berry.

6. Fuse the batting to the wrong side of each pillow top.

7. Hem the backs of the pillows by folding in the $12\frac{1}{2}$" or $16\frac{1}{2}$" edge of each piece $\frac{1}{8}$" and then another $\frac{1}{4}$". Topstitch close to the first fold for a clean, finished hem.

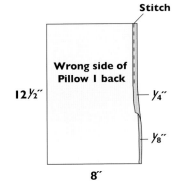

Stitch

Wrong side of Pillow I back

$12\frac{1}{2}$"

$\frac{1}{4}$"

$\frac{1}{8}$"

8"

Fold under $\frac{1}{8}$" and then $\frac{1}{4}$" and stitch.

8. Lay a pillow top right side up. Place one pillow back section on top, with right sides together, with raw edges matching on 3 sides. Part of the pillow front will still be exposed. Cover the exposed area with the second pillow back. The 2 hemmed edges will overlap by approximately $2\frac{1}{2}$".

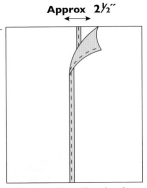

Approx $2\frac{1}{2}$"

Overlap the pillow backs.

9. Stitch $\frac{1}{4}$" from the edge of the pillow all around through all layers. Trim the corners diagonally. Turn the pillow right side out. Press. Insert the pillow form through the opening in the pillow back.

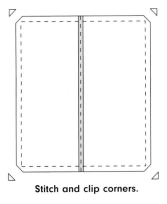

Stitch and clip corners.

Varying the Palette. Small prints and a floral print background give a totally different look for Pillow 2.

Butterfly Tote

15" x 14"

Decorative fabric tote bags are fun to make in colors that coordinate with your wardrobe. Vintage-style cottons were used for this bag to create a retro look. For a totally different approach, try a batik with a subtle design for the background fabric to give your tote a more contemporary flair. The tote features an inside double pocket and can be made with either short fabric handles, as shown, or shoulder straps.

Materials

$^7/_8$ yard for tote and inside pocket

$^2/_3$ yard for lining, handles, and large wings

$^1/_4$ yard for top accent band and butterfly body

3 assorted 4" x 6" pieces for small wings

24" x 45" fusible batting

$^1/_3$ yard lightweight fusible web

$^1/_4$ yard stabilizer for machine appliqué

Black Jeans Stitch thread

Embroidery floss in contrasting color for eyes and antennae

Large sew-on snap ($^3/_8$" or $^1/_2$")

Cutting

FABRIC	CUT
Tote	Two 15$^1/_2$" x 16$^1/_2$" rectangles
Inside pocket	One 12" x 16$^1/_2$" rectangle
Lining	Two 15$^1/_2$" x 16$^1/_2$" rectangles
Short handles*	Two 3" x 16" rectangles
Shoulder straps*	Two 3" x 40" strips (pieced)
Top accent band	One 2$^1/_2$" x 30$^1/_2$" strip

FUSIBLE BATTING	CUT
Tote	Two 15$^1/_2$" x 16$^1/_2$" rectangles
Short handles*	Two 1" x 16" rectangles
Shoulder straps*	Two 1" x 40" strips
Top accent band	One 2" x 32$^1/_2$" strip

*Note: Cut fabric and batting for either the short handles or the shoulder straps.

FABRIC PICKS

COMBINATION 1

    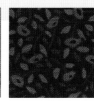 

COMBINATION 2

COMBINATION 3

    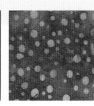 

Preparing the Appliqués

1. Using butterfly patterns A–E on pages 56–57, trace 1 each of A, A reversed, B, B reversed, C, C reversed, D, D reversed, and E onto the paper side of the fusible web. Group pieces that will be cut from the same fabric.

2. Loosely cut out the pieces and fuse them to the wrong sides of the appropriate butterfly fabrics.

3. Cut out the butterfly appliqués on the drawn lines and remove the paper backing.

4. To compose the butterfly, refer to the Appliqué Placement diagram. Arrange the appliqués right side up, in alphabetical order, on an appliqué pressing sheet. Press to fuse the overlapping pieces. Let cool. You will now be able to handle the butterfly as a single unit.

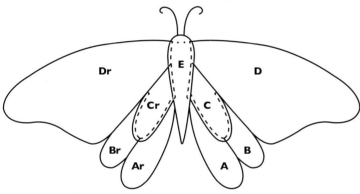

r = reversed pattern

Assembly

1. Fuse a batting rectangle to the wrong side of each tote rectangle.
2. Center the butterfly appliqué on the tote front, 3¹/₂" from the top edge. Fuse in place.

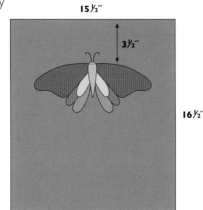

15½"

3½"

16½"

Appliqué Placement

3. Outline each appliqué shape with machine blanket stitch, using black Jeans Stitch thread. Add French knots for the butterfly eyes and embroider the antennae with a stem stitch.

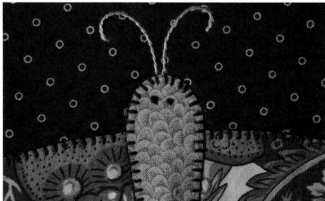

Blanket stitch appliqué, **Palette combination 1**

Blanket stitch appliqué, **Palette combination 2**

EMBROIDERY DETAILS

French Knot

Bring the needle up where you want the knot. Wrap the floss around the needle 2 or 3 times. Holding the floss tight, insert the needle back down, close to the first needle hole. Pull the needle through to the back of the fabric.

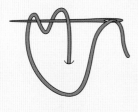

Stem Stitch

Begin by bringing the needle up at A. Insert the needle at B and bring it up again at C. Continue by inserting the needle at D and up at E. Repeat to the end of the design line.

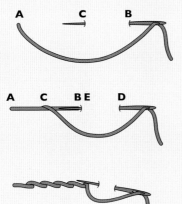

4. Place the 2 tote pieces right sides together. Stitch the sides and bottom together with a $1/4$" seam, leaving the top edge open. Press the seams open.

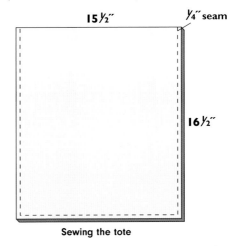

15½"   ¼" seam

16½"

Sewing the tote

5. Open and then refold 1 lower corner, keeping right sides together, so that the side and bottom seams align. Starting at the point, measure along the seam for $1\frac{1}{2}$". Mark a line perpendicular to the seam. Stitch along the marked line. Box out the remaining corner in the same way.

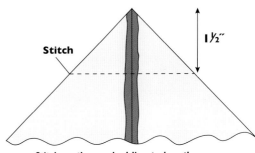

Stitch   1½"

Stitch on the marked line to box the corner

6. Fold the 12" x $16\frac{1}{2}$" pocket rectangle in half, with right sides together. Stitch $1/4$" from the shorter edges. Turn right side out and press.

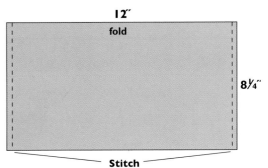

12"
fold
8¼"
Stitch

7. Place the pocket on 1 lining rectangle. Center the pocket approximately 2" in from each side and have the raw edge 6$\frac{1}{2}$" from the 15$\frac{1}{2}$" end of the lining. Stitch $\frac{1}{4}$" from the raw edges. Fold the pocket onto the lining and press. Stitch each side edge of the pocket to the lining. Stitch down the middle to divide the pocket in two.

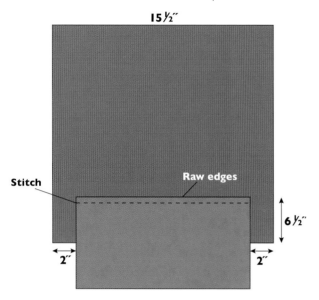

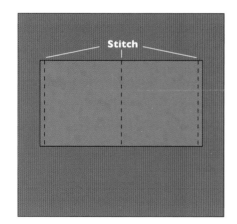

Stitching the pocket

8. Repeat Step 4 to sew the 2 lining rectangles together. Repeat Step 5 to box out the corners. Fold and press the top raw edge of the lining $\frac{3}{8}$" to the wrong side.

9. Center the batting strip on the top accent band fabric. Fuse in place. Stitch the short ends of the band trim together to make a ring. Press the seam open. Bring the raw edges together, with wrong sides facing, and press. Pin the raw edges to the top outside edge of the tote, aligning the seam with a side seam of the tote. Stitch $\frac{1}{4}$" from the edge all around.

10. To make either the short handles or the shoulder straps, place a batting strip on a handle strip, $\frac{1}{4}$" from the edge. Fuse in place. Fold the handle lengthwise in half, concealing the batting. Press. Unfold the handle. Press each long edge $\frac{1}{4}$" to the inside. Refold and pin. Stitch $\frac{1}{8}$" from each long edge. Repeat to make a second handle.

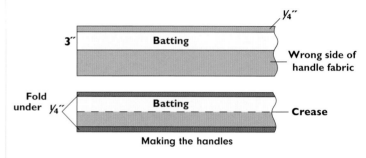

Making the handles

11. Fold the accent band down against the outside of the tote. Mark the center of the top front edge with a pin. Measure 4" from the pin in each direction and pin the handle. Stitch the handles to the tote, even with the previous stitching. Attach a handle to the tote back in the same way.

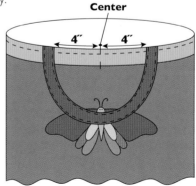

Attaching the handles

12. Fold up the accent band. Insert the lining into the tote, wrong sides together, with the pocket at the back. Pin in place. The lining should cover the seam allowance of the accent band. On the outside, stitch in-the-ditch between the trim and the tote. Hand sew a snap to the inside edges of the accent band for a center closure.

Top inside of tote where accent band and handle join

Palette combination 2

49" x 53¹/₂"

Let Baby snuggle under this crib quilt or hang it on the wall. Make this sweet quilt in realistic animal print colors or in soft pastels. Either way, you'll have fun assembling the fabric palette. The animal appliqués are fun on their own and can be used to make other nursery accessories, such as a chair cushion, a carry-along tote bag, pillows, or even curtains.

Materials

1/3 yard for zebra background*

1/3 yard for lion background*

1/3 yard for elephant background*

1/2 yard for giraffe background*

1 1/4 yards for sashing, borders, and binding*

1/4 yard for zebras

1/8 yard or scraps for zebra manes and tails

1/4 yard for lions

1/8 yard or scraps for lion manes

1/4 yard for elephants

1/8 yard for elephant heads and trunks

3/8 yard for giraffes

3 yards for backing

53" x 58" batting

3 yards lightweight fusible web

2 3/8 yards stabilizer for machine appliqué

Thread to match appliqués

Note: If the fabric you choose is less than 42" wide, you will need to purchase extra to piece the background or borders. For backgrounds, purchase 1 1/4 yards of fabric to cut lengthwise and avoid piecing.

Cutting

FABRIC	CUT
Zebra background	One 8" x 41 1/2" rectangle
Lion background	One 7 1/2" x 41 1/2" rectangle
Elephant background	One 9 1/2" x 41 1/2" rectangle
Giraffe background	One 15" x 41 1/2" rectangle
Sashing	Three 3" x 41 1/2" strips*
Top/bottom borders	Two 4 1/2" x 54" strips*
Side borders	Two 4 1/2" x 46" strips*
Single-fold binding	Six 1 1/2" x 40" strips

Note: Cut crosswise and piece as necessary.

FABRIC PICKS

COMBINATION 1

COMBINATION 2

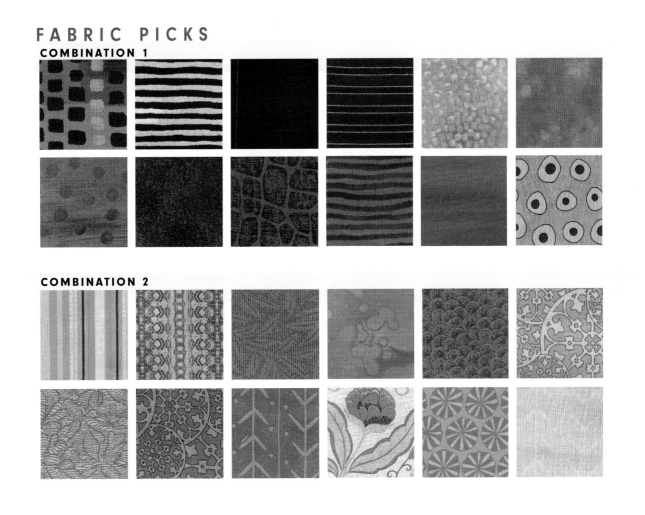

Preparing the Appliqués

1. Using the animal patterns A–K on pages 59–62, trace 4 zebras, 3 lions, 4 elephants, and 5 giraffes onto the paper side of the fusible web. Group pieces that will be cut from the same fabric.

2. Loosely cut out the pieces and fuse them to the wrong side of the corresponding fabrics. Cut out all the appliqués on the drawn lines and remove the paper backing.

Assembly

Refer to the quilt photograph on page 36 for appliqué placement. Place the animal appliqués on the background pieces, evenly spaced, allowing for $1/4$" seams at the top, bottom, and side edges. Do a dry run to double-check the placement before fusing.

1. Arrange zebras on the 8" x $41^1/2$" background. Fuse the tail and mane first, then the zebra body.

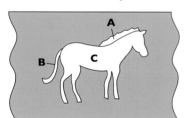

Zebra Appliqué Placement

2. Arrange the lions on the $7^1/2$" x $41^1/2$" background fabric. Fuse the legs, body, and head first, then the mane.

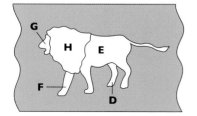

Lion Appliqué Placement

3. Arrange the elephants on the $9^1/2$" x $41^1/2$" background fabric. Fuse the body first, then the head.

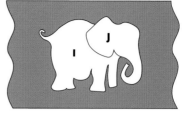

Elephant Appliqué Placement

4. Arrange the giraffes on the 15" x $41^1/2$" background fabric. Fuse in place.

Giraffe Appliqué Placement

5. With stabilizer behind the background fabrics, use matching thread to outline each shape with satin stitch.

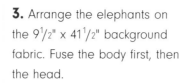
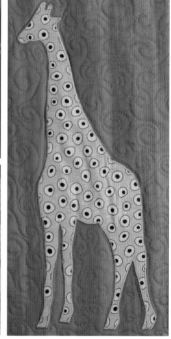

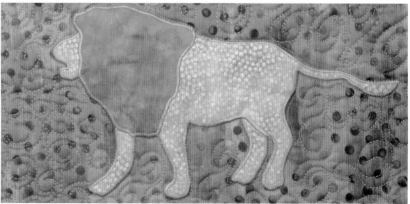

Satin stitched appliqués

6. Arrange the appliquéd panels and sashing strips as shown in the Assembly Diagram. Stitch a sashing strip to the bottom edge of the zebra panel, using a $^1/_4$" seam. Press toward the sashing. Stitch the lion panel to the bottom edge of the sashing. Press toward the sashing. Continue until all the panels and sashing strips are joined.

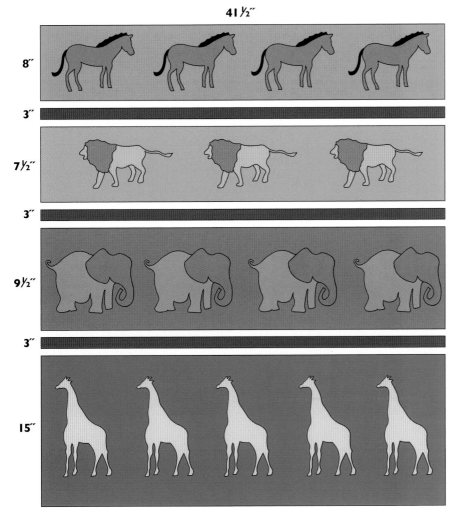

Assembly Diagram

7. Stitch a side border to each side edge of the quilt top. Press toward the border. Add the top and bottom borders. Press toward the borders.

A Note About Binding

Because I prefer a single-fold binding, I cut strips $1^1/2$" wide for a finished binding width of approximately $^3/8$". If you want double-fold binding, cut strips 2" to $2^1/2$" wide, depending on how wide you want your finished binding to be. The yardages have been calculated using $2^1/2$" wide strips, so you should have adequate fabric.

Finishing

1. Piece the backing fabric with a horizontal seam. Place the backing wrong side up on a table or smooth surface. Place the batting on top and smooth out any wrinkles. Center the quilt top right side up on the batting.

2. Hand baste the quilt sandwich with large running stitches, or use rustproof safety pins if you will be machine quilting.

3. Quilt by hand or machine. Outline quilt around the animals to make them stand out. The background was quilted with swirls to create a playful look (see the quilting design on page 40). The borders were echo-quilted.

4. Trim the excess batting and backing even with the quilt top.

5. Use a diagonal seam to join the strips for binding end-to-end. Press the seams open.

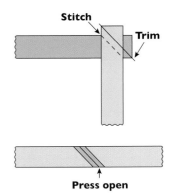

6. Press over a long raw edge of the binding strip $^1/_4$" to the wrong side. Align the other raw edge even with the edge of the quilt, with right sides together. Pin the binding to the edge of the quilt a few inches from the corner. Leave the first few inches of the binding unattached. Begin sewing, using a $^1/_4$" seam allowance.

7. Stop $^1/_4$" from the first corner, and backstitch. Lift the presser foot and needle.

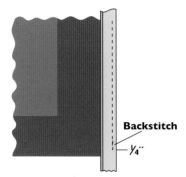

Backstitch

$^1/_4$"

8. Rotate the quilt $^1/_4$ turn. Fold the binding at a right angle so it extends straight above the quilt. Then bring the binding strip down even with the edge of the quilt and begin sewing at the folded edge.

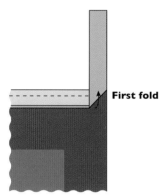

First fold

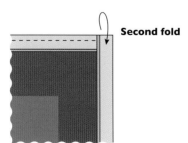

Second fold

9. Continue sewing around the quilt. Repeat Steps 7 and 8 for all the corners.

10. When you reach the last side, fold under the beginning end of the binding strip $^1/_4$". Continue stitching about 1" beyond the edge where you started. Clip the threads, remove the quilt from the machine, and trim the excess binding.

11. Fold the binding over the raw edges to the backing and hand stitch the binding to the quilt, mitering the corners as you come to them.

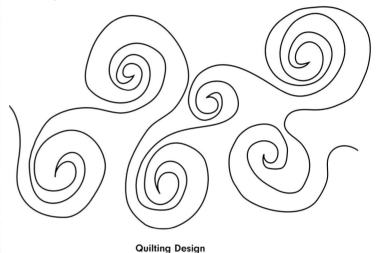

Quilting Design

Garden Chair Cushion

10" x 17" chair cushion

Wooden chairs are much more comfortable when the back is covered with a pad. This decorative cushion made of bright batiks speaks of a garden landscape with brilliant summer colors. It can easily be sized wider or longer to fit your chair (see Sized to Fit on page 44, and purchase extra fabrics as needed). This is a great way to dress up wooden folding chairs.

Materials

$^1/_8$ yard blue batik for background

$^5/_8$ yard black solid for background and backing

$^1/_8$ yard each of 3 different green batiks for stems, leaves, and mountains

$^1/_8$ yard each of 1 pink, 1 yellow, and 1 purple batik for appliqués

$^1/_8$ yard melon batik for appliqués and sashing

10" x 17" fusible batting

$^1/_2$ yard lightweight fusible web

$^1/_2$ yard tear-away stabilizer

Thread to match appliqués

$1^1/_2$ yards grosgrain ribbon, about 1" wide

Cutting

FABRIC	CUT
Landscape background	One 3" x 10$^1/_2$" rectangle
Flowers background	One 10$^1/_2$" x 11" piece
Squares background	One 3$^1/_2$" x 10$^1/_2$" rectangle
Sashing	Two 1" x 10$^1/_2$" strips
Backing	One 10$^1/_2$" x 17" piece

Preparing the Appliqués

1. Use the landscape and flower patterns A–L on pages 57–58. Trace the patterns onto fusible web. Group pieces that will be cut from the same fabric. Use a pencil and ruler to draw 14 squares onto fusible web, each 1" x 1", to be cut from assorted fabrics.

FABRIC PICKS
COMBINATION 1

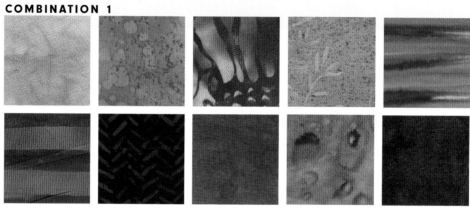

COMBINATION 2

2. Loosely cut out the pieces and fuse them to the wrong side of the appropriate fabrics.

3. Cut out the appliqué shapes on the drawn lines and remove the paper backing.

Assembly

1. Place appliqués A, B, and C on the 3" x 10^1/$_2$" landscape background. Overlap the pieces as shown. Do a dry run to double-check the placement before fusing the pieces in alphabetical order.

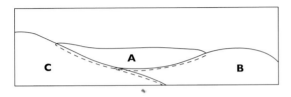

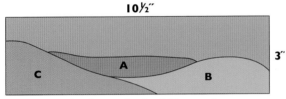

Landscape Appliqué Placement

2. Place the flower, stem, and leaf appliqués on the 10^1/$_2$" x 11" background. Check your placement, and then fuse each flower in numerical order.

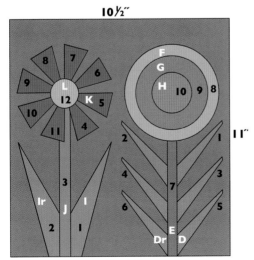

Flower Appliqué Placement

3. Arrange the assorted square appliqués on the 3^1/$_2$" x 10^1/$_2$" background. Space them equally, allowing for a ^{1}/$_4$" seam allowance all around. Fuse the pieces in place.

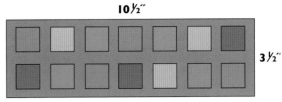

Squares Appliqué Placement

4. Satin stitch the appliqués in place. Use a tear-away stabilizer behind the pieces to prevent stretching and puckering. Refer to Satin Stitch on page 17.

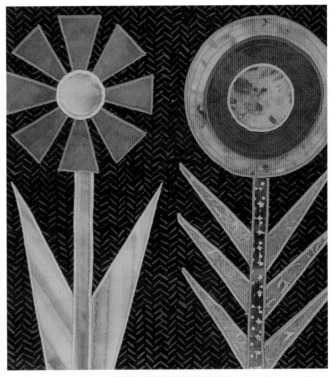

Stitching details

5. Arrange the appliquéd panels and sashing strips as shown in the Assembly Diagram. Stitch the pieces together with ¹/₄" seams, pressing toward the sashing after each addition.

8. Cut the grosgrain ribbon into two 27" lengths. Fold the ribbons in half and tack to the back of the cushion at the upper corners.

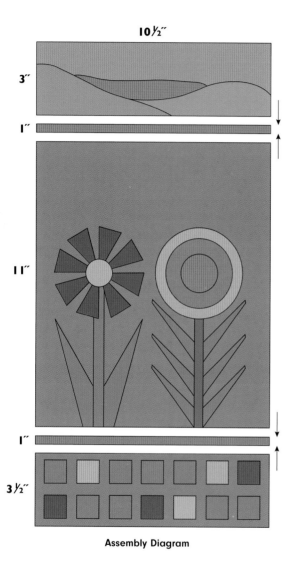

Assembly Diagram

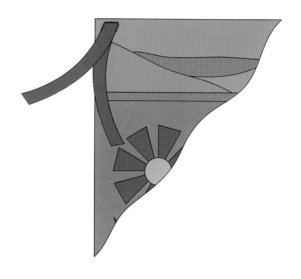

Ribbon ties

6. Center the 10" x 17" piece of batting on the reverse side of the appliquéd panel, so that ¹/₄" of fabric extends all around. Fuse in place.

7. Place the appliquéd panel and backing right sides together. Stitch ¹/₄" from the edge all around, leaving a 5" opening in the bottom for turning. Trim the corners. Turn the work right side out. Fold in the seam allowance at the opening and press. Slipstitch closed.

Sized to Fit

1. Measure the width of the chair back across the top (width).
2. Measure the height from the top to the seat (length).
3. On graph paper, draw a rectangle that measures the width x length.

4. Cut out the graph paper shape. Place it against the chair back to check the fit. Adjust the dimensions as needed.
5. Mark and cut the graph paper pattern into 3 background panels and 2 horizontal sashing strips, using the Assembly Diagram at left as a guide.
6. Use the patterns to cut the background fabrics and sashing. Remember to add a ¹/₄" seam allowance to all the edges.
7. Adjust the appliqué patterns and the squares to fit your background pieces.

Floral Table Runner

15" x 36"

These large floral appliqués came straight from a printed fabric. Become a detective as you shop for printed fabrics—you never know when you might come across an interesting pattern that could double as an appliqué. The leaves in this fabric were too fussy to use as is, so I traced them and then simplified the shape. I've included my pattern in case it will work with your flower.

Materials

$1/2$ yard neutral for background

$1/2$ yard large floral print for appliqués

$1/2$ yard contrasting large floral print for appliqués

$1/2$ yard green for leaves and binding

$1/2$ yard fabric for backing

15" x 36" fusible batting

1 yard lightweight fusible web

Thread to match appliqués

Light green thread for embroidery details

FABRIC PICKS

COMBINATION 1

COMBINATION 2

Cutting

FABRIC	CUT
Background	One 15" x 36" piece
Backing	One 15" x 36" piece
Binding	Three $1^{1}/2$" x 40" strips

Palette combination 2

Preparing the Appliqués

1. Select 7 flowers, each about 6" across, from the floral print to use as appliqués.

Floral Design

Be creative, as when arranging a bouquet of fresh flowers. Vary the design according to the size and shape of the flowers in your fabric. If your flowers are smaller, use more of them as appliqués in your design.

2. Cut out each flower about 1" beyond the edge of the design. Cut a piece of fusible web the same size. Fuse the adhesive to the wrong side of each flower, using a pressing sheet to prevent sticking. Let cool. Cut out each flower, simplifying the shape as desired.

3. Use the leaf pattern on page 55, if desired, and trace 12 leaves (6 in reverse) onto fusible web. Using a pencil and ruler, draw 4 stems, $^1/_2$" x 8". Loosely cut out the designs and fuse them to the wrong side of the green fabric. Let cool. Cut out the leaves and stems on the drawn lines.

Assembly

1. Fuse the batting to the wrong side of the background fabric.

2. Turn the background fabric right side up. Insert 2 pins on each long edge, 12" apart, to visually divide the background into 3 sections.

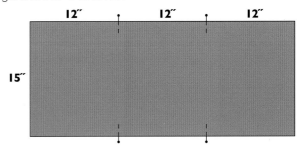

3. Place 3 flower appliqués in the middle section, overlapping the petals as shown or as needed for your design. Tuck 2 pairs of leaves around the flowers.

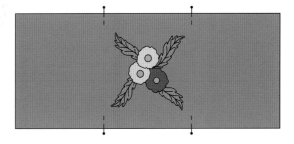

4. Fit the remaining floral appliqués in the 2 end sections. Give each flower its own stem and leaves. Adjust the entire layout as desired. Fuse the pieces in place, working from the background to the foreground.

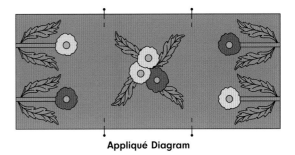

Appliqué Diagram

5. Machine-appliqué the edges of the stems and leaves in satin stitch first. Repeat for the flowers.

6. Fit the machine with an open-toe embroidery foot or a darning foot. Add decorative machine embroidery stitching in the stems and leaves. Follow the printed design to outline some of the inner petals, and work in details like the pistil and stamens. Use light green thread to stitch veins and other details in the leaves and stems.

7. Refer to Finishing on pages 39–40 of *Animals on Parade*. Layer the appliquéd panel with the backing fabric, wrong sides together, and baste with thread or pins. Quilt around the floral designs by hand or machine, and bind the edges.

Satin stitch

Flowers

Leaf veins

Moonlit Mountains

39" x 24"

A few triangles and a circle and—presto!—you have an instant mountain landscape. The edges of the appliqués are folded back against the freezer paper patterns and sewn with invisible stitch. The resulting edges are clean and sharp, giving this design a decided graphic edge. Make the wallhanging as shown, or make several as blocks and then set them together to make a larger wallhanging.

Materials

$1/2$ yard for sky background

$1/4$ yard for inner border

$1^1/2$ yards for outer border, backing, and binding

$3/8$ yard for mountain A

$3/8$ yard for mountain B

$3/8$ yard for mountain C

8" x 8" square for moon

Scraps for corner squares

29" x 44" batting

Monofilament thread

Freezer paper

Washable glue stick

Cutting

FABRIC	CUT
Sky background	One $17^1/2$" x $32^1/2$" rectangle
Side inner borders	Two 1" x $17^1/2$" strips
Top and bottom inner borders	Two 1" x $32^1/2$" strips
Inner border corner squares	Four 1" x 1" squares
Top and bottom outer borders	Two $3^1/2$" x $40^1/2$" strips
Side outer borders	Two $3^1/2$" x $25^1/2$" strips
Binding	Four $1^1/2$" x 42" strips

Preparing the Appliqués

1. Use a ruler and pencil to draw mountain patterns A, B, and C on freezer paper. Mark the base of each triangle so you will know which is the bottom.

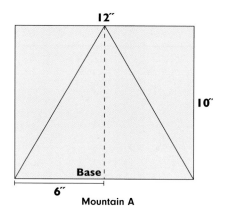

12″

10″

Base

6″

Mountain A

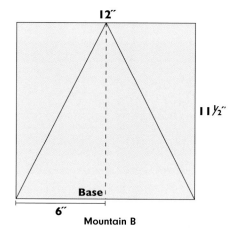

12″

$11^1/2$″

Base

6″

Mountain B

FABRIC PICKS

COMBINATION 1

COMBINATION 2

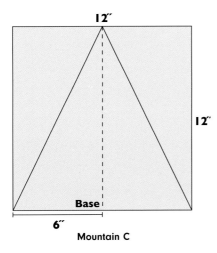

12″

12″

Base

6″

Mountain C

2. Use a compass to draw a 7"-diameter circle on freezer paper (or trace around a 7" salad plate). Label as D.

3. Cut out freezer paper templates A, B, C, and D. Place each template shiny side down on the wrong side of the corresponding fabric. Press to fuse. Cut the fabric $^1/_4$" beyond the edge of the template all around. Do not remove the paper.

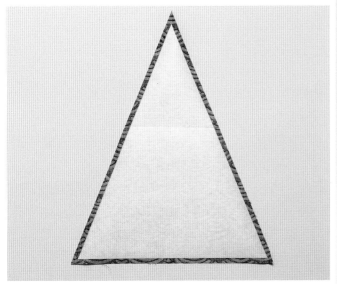

Cutting a mountain

4. Place mountain A paper side up. Run a glue stick around the edge, catching both the edge of the paper template and the fabric seam allowance. Use your fingertips to fold and press the seam allowance onto the paper template. Repeat for pieces B, C, and D.

Assembly

1. Arrange the moon and mountains on the sky background, as shown in the photo on page 49 and in the Appliqué Diagram on page 52. Pin the moon in place and remove the mountains.

2. Sew an invisible stitch around the edge of the moon with monofilament thread. (See Invisible Stitch on page 21.)

3. Turn over the work. Using scissors, carefully trim the background fabric from the moon area to within $^1/_2$" of the stitching line. Wet the fabric. When the freezer paper is sufficiently pliable, remove it. Press from the wrong side to dry the fabric. Press again on the right side.

Wrong side

4. Repeat Steps 1–3 to appliqué mountains A, B, and C to the sky background. Appliqué A first, then B and C.

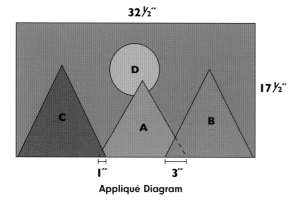

Appliqué Diagram

5. Sew the side inner borders to the appliquéd panel. Press toward the borders. Sew a corner square to each end of the top and bottom inner borders. Press toward the corner squares. Add these borders to the panel. Press.

6. Lay 1 outer border strip wrong side up. Measure $3^{1}/_{4}$" from each end and insert a pin. Pin the strip to the panel, with right sides together. Match the pins to the $^{1}/_{4}$" stitching line at each corner. Stitch between the pins. Press the seams toward the borders.

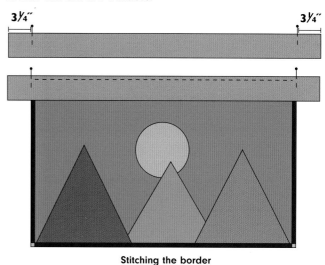

Stitching the border

7. Repeat Step 6 for each border. The excess will hang loose at the corners.

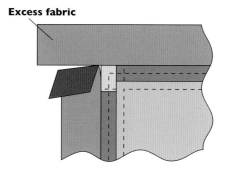

8. Press from the right side. Let 1 border overlap the other at each corner. Fold under the top strip, making a 45° angle from the inside corner to the outer corner. Press.

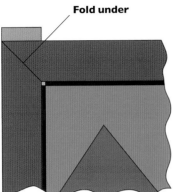

Fold under

9. Fold the quilt back on itself, with right sides together, and pin the 2 border strips together. Stitch along the fold line. Check the right side to see if the miter seam is straight and lies flat. Trim the seam allowance to $1/4$". Press the seam allowance to one side. Repeat to miter all 4 corners.

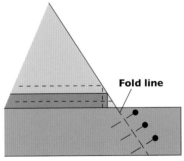

Fold line

Stitch on fold line.

10. Layer and baste the quilt top, batting, and backing. Quilt simple landscape contours by hand or machine. Bind the edges. Refer to Finishing on pages 39–40 for additional details.

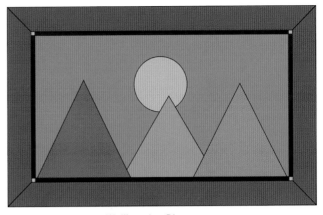

Wallhanging Diagram

Patterns

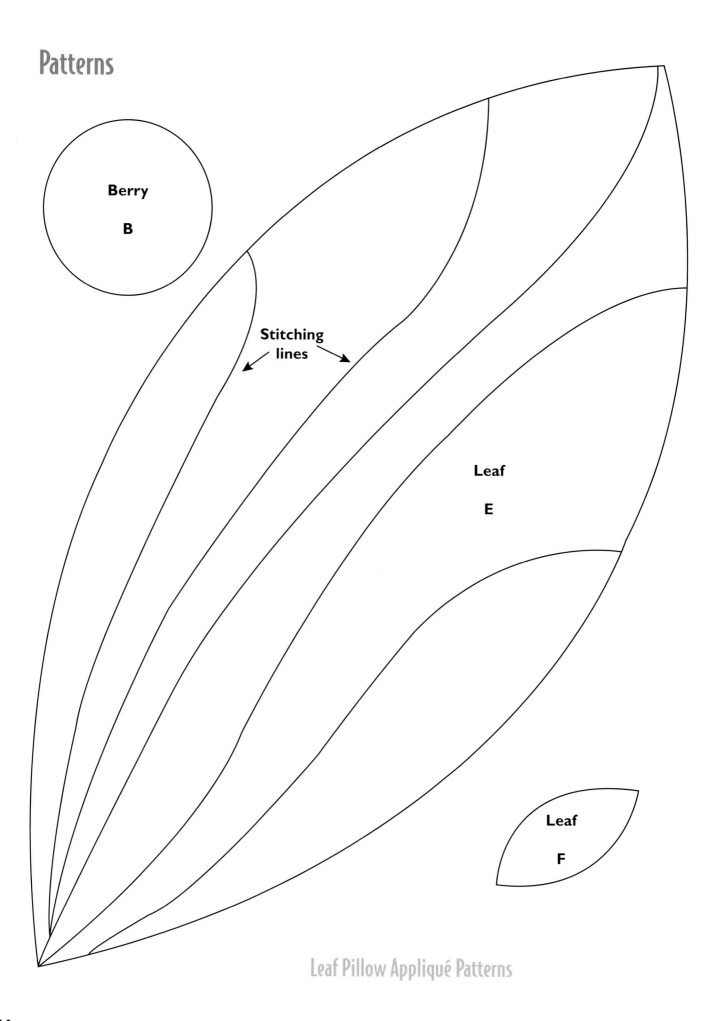

Berry

B

Stitching
lines

Leaf

E

Leaf

F

Leaf Pillow Appliqué Patterns

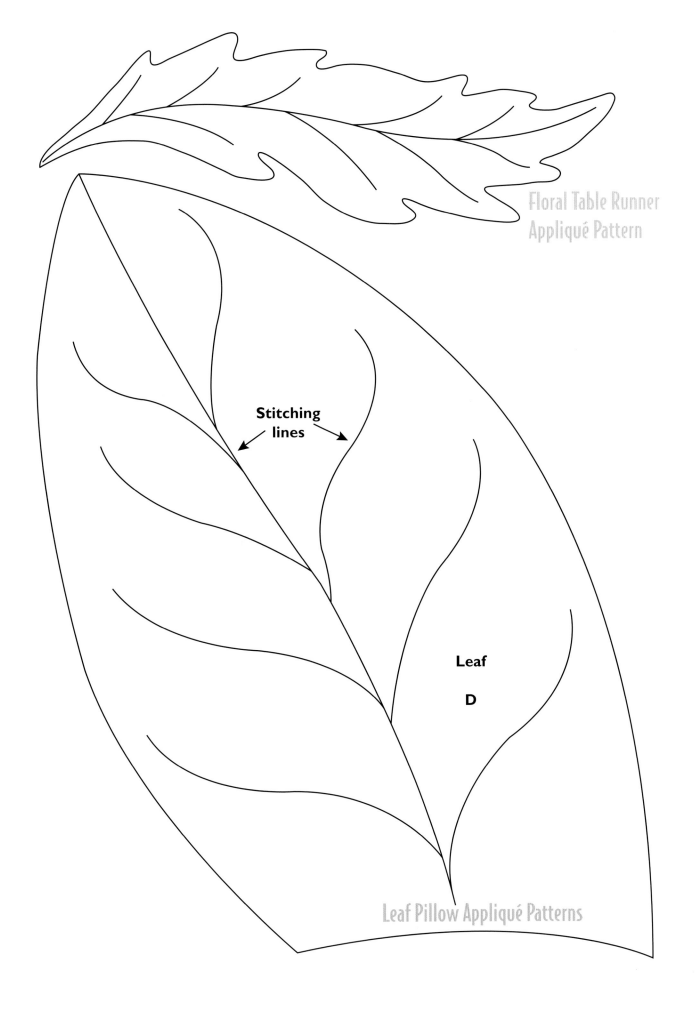

Floral Table Runner
Appliqué Pattern

Stitching
lines

Leaf

D

Leaf Pillow Appliqué Patterns

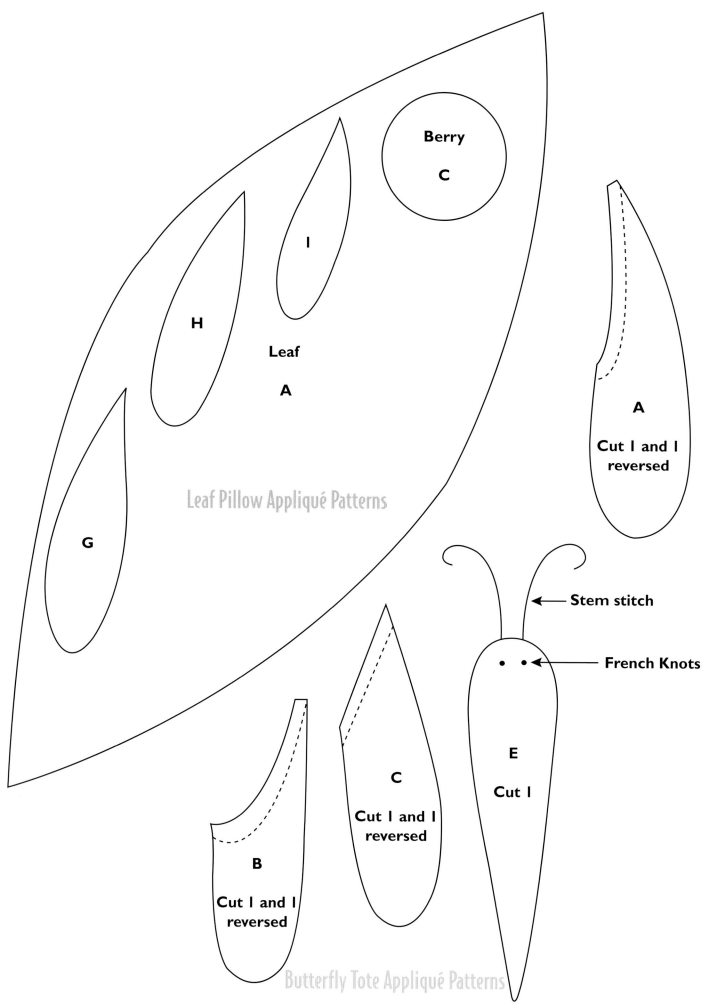

Berry

C

I

H

Leaf

A

Leaf Pillow Appliqué Patterns

G

A

Cut 1 and 1 reversed

Stem stitch

French Knots

E

Cut 1

B

Cut 1 and 1 reversed

C

Cut 1 and 1 reversed

Butterfly Tote Appliqué Patterns

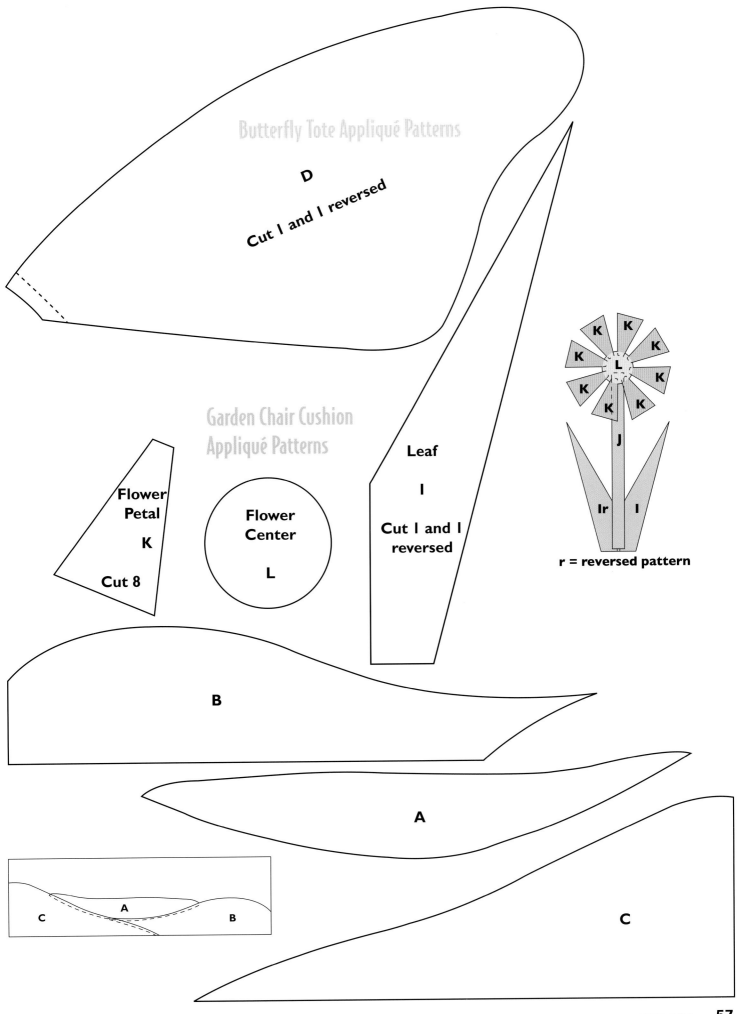

Butterfly Tote Appliqué Patterns

D

Cut I and I reversed

Garden Chair Cushion
Appliqué Patterns

Flower
Petal

K

Cut 8

Flower
Center

L

Leaf

I

Cut I and I
reversed

K K K K K K K K
L
J
Ir I

r = reversed pattern

B

A

C

A
B

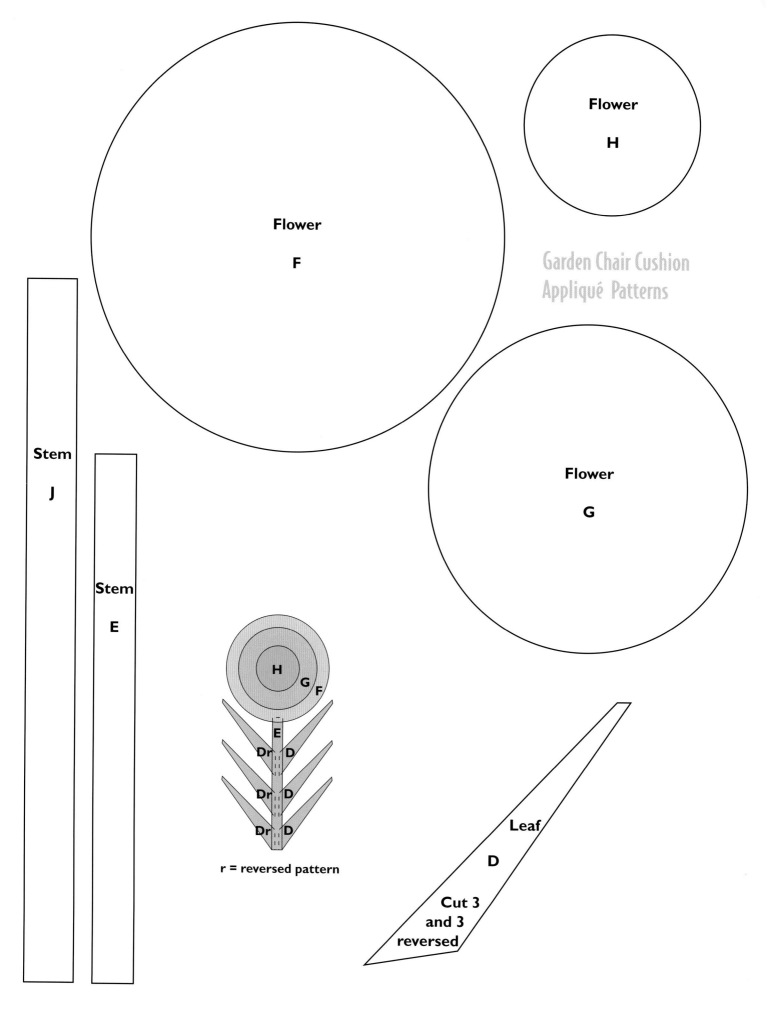

Flower

F

Flower

H

Garden Chair Cushion
Appliqué Patterns

Flower

G

Stem

J

Stem

E

H G F

E

Dr D

Dr D

Dr D

r = reversed pattern

Leaf

D

**Cut 3
and 3
reversed**

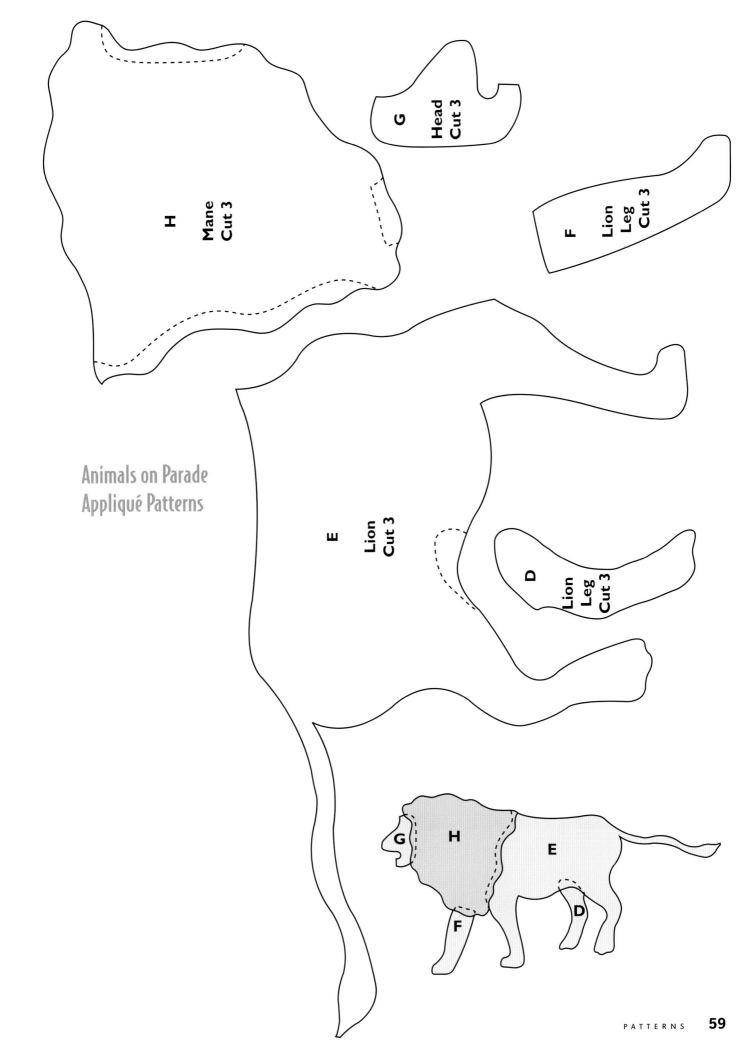

G
Head
Cut 3

H
Mane
Cut 3

F
Lion
Leg
Cut 3

Animals on Parade
Appliqué Patterns

E
Lion
Cut 3

D
Lion
Leg
Cut 3

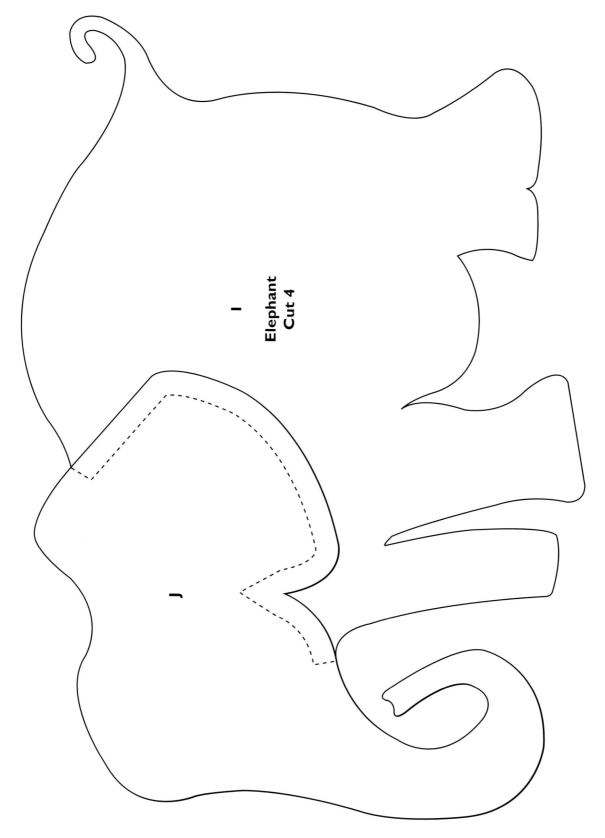

I

**Elephant
Cut 4**

Animals on Parade Appliqué Patterns

Join to body at dashed line.

Join to head at dashed line.

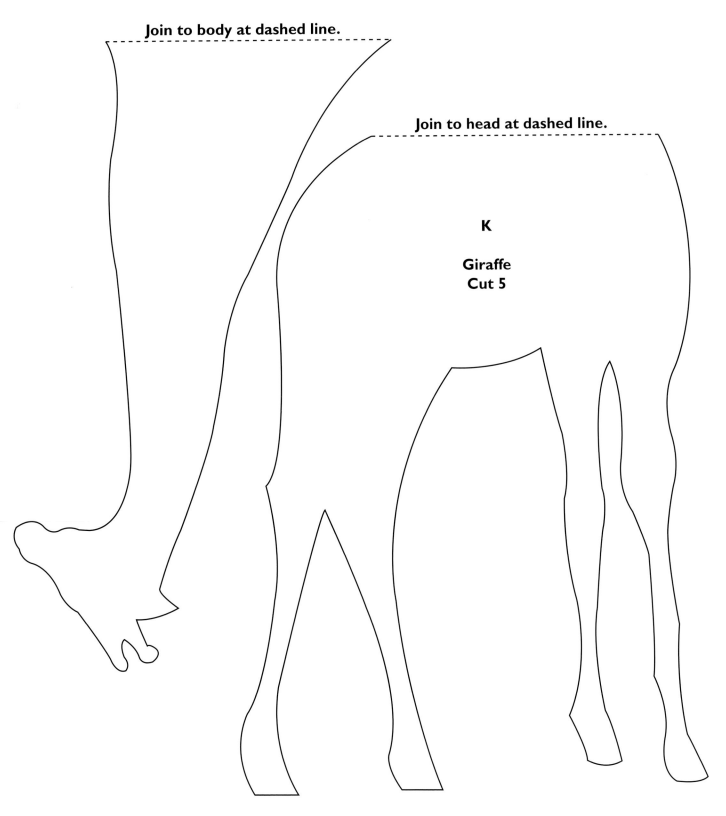

K

Giraffe
Cut 5

Animals on Parade Appliqué Patterns

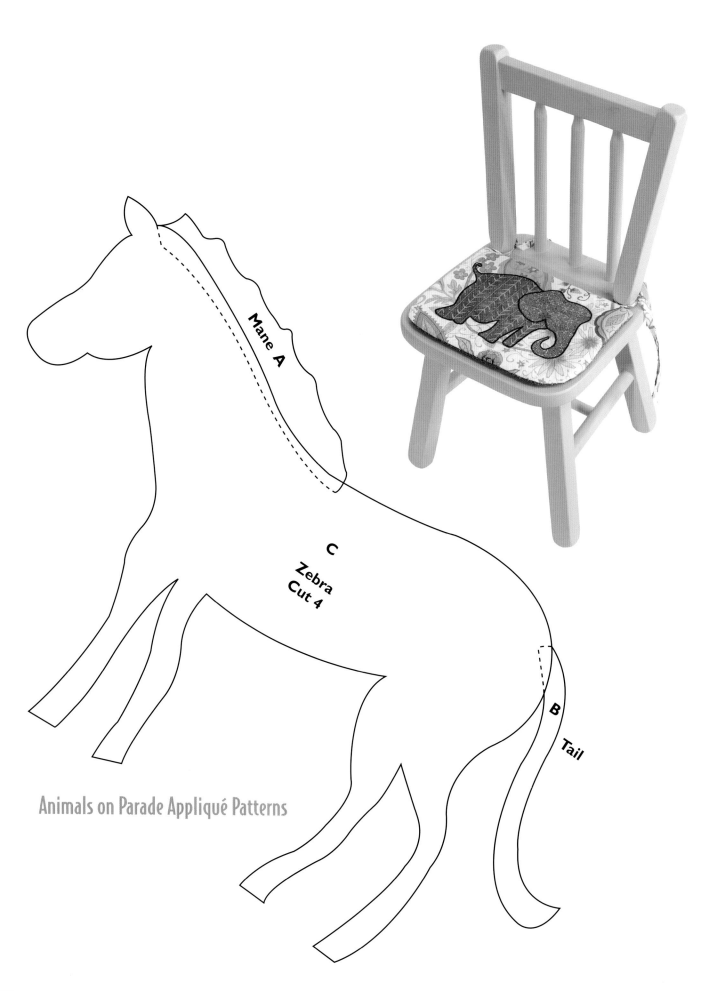

Mane A

C

Zebra
Cut 4

B

Tail

Animals on Parade Appliqué Patterns

About the Author

Jean Wells has written 24 quilting books in almost as many years. Her friendly teaching style and love of color are a constant, whether she's covering the basics in her book *Patchwork Quilts Made Easy* or collaborating with daughter Valori Wells on a specialty title like *Garden-Inspired Quilts*. As owner of The Stitchin' Post in Sisters, Oregon, Jean is in close contact with quilters of all levels, a connection she relies on for new ideas and inspiration. Jean has been featured in numerous magazines, has appeared as a guest on many TV shows, and has traveled the world teaching others the joys of quilting. At home, she looks forward to organizing the Sisters' Annual Outdoor Quilt Show, held the second Saturday in July, or simply puttering in her garden, coming up with more patchwork patterns to plant.

Quilting Supplies

The Stitchin' Post
P.O. Box 280
311 West Cascade
Sisters, OR 97759
541-549-6061
www.stitchinpost.com

Cotton Patch Mail Order
3405 Hall Lane, Dept. CTB
Lafayette, CA 94595
800-835-4418
www.quiltusa@yahoo.com

Other books by Jean Wells

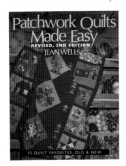

Patchwork Quilts Made Easy
Revised, 2nd Edition
33 Quilt Favorites, Old & New
by Jean Wells

Garden-Inspired Quilts
Design Journals for 12 Quilt
Projects
by Jean & Valori Wells

Through the Garden Gate
Quilters and Their Gardens
by Jean & Valori Wells

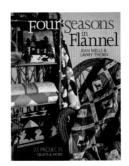

Four Seasons in Flannel
23 Projects—Quilts & More
by Jean Wells & Lawry Thorn

Index